REGIONS OF THE WORLD

Middle and South America

Mark Stewart

Heinemann Library
Chicago, Illinois

Customer Service 888-454-2279
Visit our Web site at:
www.heinemannraintree.com

Editorial: Andrew Farrow and Robyn Hardyman
Design: Steve Mead and Q2A Creative
Illustrations: International Mapping Associates, Inc
Picture Research: Melissa Allison and Kay Altwegg

Originated by Chroma Graphics (Overseas) Pte. Ltd
Printed and Bound in China

12 11 10 09 08
10 9 8 7 6 5 4 3 2 1

ISBNs: 978-1-4034-9897-7 (hardcover)
        978-1-4034-9906-6 (paperback)

Library of Congress Cataloging-in-Publication Data

Stewart, Mark, 1960-
  Middle and South America / Mark Stewart.
     p. cm. -- (Regions of the world)
  Includes bibliographical references and index.
  ISBN-13: 978-1-4034-9897-7 (hc)
  ISBN-13: 978-1-4034-9906-6 (pb)
  1. Latin America--Juvenile literature. I. Title.
  F1408.2.S74 2007
  980--dc22

                              2007011620

Acknowledgments
The publishers would like to thank the following for
permission to reproduce copyrighted material:

© Alamy (Danita Delimont) **25, 40** (Sue Cunningham
Photographic) **47** (Adrian Lascom) **55** (Barry Lewis) **10**
(Frances M. Roberts) **34** (Gustavo Oramas/CI96CA) **42**
(Jacques Jangoux) **4, 21** (Jon Arnold Images) **30, 48**
(SCPhotos) **53**; © Brand X pictures/Philip Coblentz **17**;
© Corbis (Jon Hicks) **36** (Tony Arruza) **44**; © FLPA/
Frans Lanting **18**; © Getty Images **16** (Image Bank)
49; © PA Photos/AP/Eduardo Verdugo **22**; © Panos
Pictures (Mark Henley) **38** (Sean Sprague) **45**; © Photo
by AKG Images. Kahlo, Frida, Coyoaca 1910 - ibid.
1954. Self-portrait with loose hair, 1947. Christie's
New York, 15/16 May 1991 © 2007 Banco de Mexico
Diego Rivera & Frida Kahlo Museums Trust. Av. Cinco
de Mayo No.2, Col. Centro, Del. Cuauhtemoc 06059,
Mexico, D.F., **39**; Robert Harding (Bruno Morandi) **33**
(David Lomax) **51** (Gavin Hellier) **32**; © Still Pictures
(Lynda Richardson) **28** (Giribas) **35**; © TIPS Images/
Sergio Jorge **27**; ©Biblioteca Nacional, Madrid,
Spain/The Bridgeman Art Library **8**; © PA photos/AP/
Aunpam Nath **21**.

Cover photograph of the statue of *Christ the
Redeemer,* in Rio de Janeiro, Brazil, reproduced with
permission of Lonely Planet Images/Ricardo Gomes.

Disclaimer
All the Internet addresses (URLs) given in this book
were valid at the time of going to press. However,
due to the dynamic nature of the Internet, some
addresses may have changed, or sites may have
changed or ceased to exist since publication. While
the author and publishers regret any inconvenience
this may cause readers, no responsibility for any such
changes can be accepted by either the author or
publishers.

Contents

Introducing Middle and South America **5**

Natural Features **11**

People **23**

Culture **31**

Natural Resources and Economy **43**

Fact File **56**

Timeline **58**

Glossary **60**

Find Out More **61**

Index **63**

Any words appearing in the text in bold, **like this**, are explained in the Glossary.

Introducing Middle and South America

Middle and South America—often called Latin America—is a vast region that includes all of South America and Central America, part of North America (Mexico), and the island nations and territories of the Caribbean. It stretches from the southern border of the United States south through the **Tropic of Cancer**, the equator, and the **Tropic of Capricorn**. The southern tip of South America is less than 700 miles (1,125 kilometers) from Antarctica. This is about the same distance between New York and Chicago, and between London, England, and Vienna, Austria.

Middle and South America make up a region of stunning diversity, from its landforms to its climates to its people. This area includes tropical rain forests, snow-capped mountains, sun-baked **deserts**, windswept coastlines, and tranquil white-sand beaches. Although most of the people in Middle and South America speak Spanish, many other tongues can be heard as one travels through the region, including Portuguese, English, French, and Dutch. There are even more **indigenous** languages, most of which date back to the time before the first European explorers arrived.

← The cities of South America often show contrasts between rich and poor, rural and urban. In Rio de Janeiro, Brazil, comfortable apartment blocks are not far from a slum, or *favela*, which rises up the hillside.

By the numbers

The countries of Middle and South America are listed, with their size, capital cities, and population numbers, on page 56. Some of the world's most populated countries are located in the region: Brazil, Mexico, Colombia, Argentina, Peru, and Venezuela. As of 2006, Brazil ranked seventh in the world with a population of about 188 million. In comparison, the population of the United States is approximately 300 million; the population of China is more than 1.3 billion.

Three of the world's largest countries are also in this region: Brazil, Argentina, and Mexico. The region's smallest country is the island nation of Anguilla, which is a territory of the United Kingdom. The smallest U.S. state, Rhode Island, is more than 30 times the size of Anguilla.

Growing cities

About two-thirds of the people in Middle and South America live in cities and towns. Some of the most populated cities in the world are located in the region. They include Buenos Aires in Argentina, São Paolo in Brazil, Mexico City in Mexico, and Lima in Peru. More than 20 million people live in **metropolitan areas** of Mexico City and São Paolo. Approximately the same number of people live in the metropolitan areas of New York City and Mumbai, India.

Every day, the cities in Middle and South America expand. As more people move from the countryside, the urban populations grow, and more land is developed for housing and industry. This trend creates

BUILD UP ... OR BUILD OUT?

The explosive growth of cities in Middle and South America has forced many governments to make hard choices. As populations increase, it makes sense to build taller office and apartment buildings that will hold more people. Unfortunately, this is not always possible. Modern construction materials and equipment can be difficult to come by, because they must be brought in from great distances. Providing energy, water, and sewage service to tall structures is not always possible either. This takes a modern and sophisticated **infrastructure**, which most towns and cities in the region do not yet have. Thus, many cities have grown "out"—with one- and two-story buildings stretching for miles. This expansion creates more pollution as people drive longer distances. It also has pushed the poor to dangerous areas on the fringes of these cities. Many people live in temporary structures built on steep slopes, where heavy rains can trigger deadly mud slides and where there is little access to sanitation and clean water.

opportunities, challenges, and concerns for the leaders in the region. Each must estimate the correct balance between land used for agriculture and land used for housing and manufacturing. Part of this balance also includes humankind's impact on the environment, as many cities in this part of the world are located close to fragile wilderness areas.

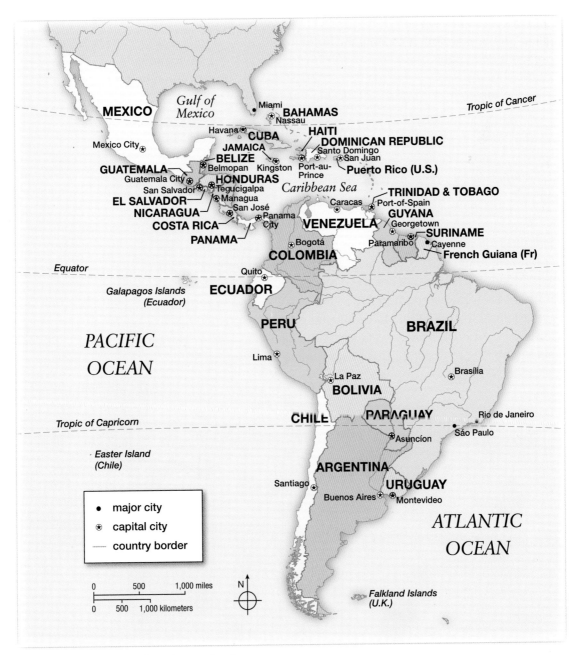

This political map shows the major countries of Middle and South America.

History of Middle and South America

The first inhabitants of Middle and South America **migrated** there from Central Asia at least 10,000 years ago. They developed highly sophisticated cultures and belief systems, and created beautiful art and architecture. Beginning in the late 1400s, the powerful nations of Europe wanted the vast resources of this region. They wanted precious metals, such as gold and silver, as well as sugar, spices, and raw materials that were not available in Europe. Spanish adventurers used their skill in warfare to conquer much of present-day Mexico and the Caribbean, and other countries soon followed. By the 1700s, most of the region was under the control of European colonists.

In 1750, Spain and Portugal signed a **treaty** dividing all of South America between them. During the early 1800s, however, many colonies, including Venezuela, Peru, and Argentina, declared their independence from these two European powers. Mexico, which was under Spanish rule, also won its freedom during this era.

The people of Middle and South America believed that they should determine the region's future. During the 20th century, many of the Caribbean islands under British and French control also declared their independence. Today, there are still many territories under foreign control in the region, including Aruba and the Netherland Antilles (Netherlands); Guadeloupe, Martinique, and French Guiana (France); Montserrat, Anguilla, Turks and Caicos, the Cayman Islands, British Virgin Islands, and Falkland Islands (United Kingdom); and the U.S. Virgin Islands and Puerto Rico (United States).

The Spanish *conquistadores* used their superior weapons to defeat the indigenous people of Middle and South America. This drawing from the 1500s shows Spaniards (left) being attacked by Aztec warriors.

FREEDOM!

The process of gaining independence in Middle and South America continues to this day. Dates given for independence vary from source to source, because a country may gain independence in one year but not set up its own government until later. Also, the newly independent country and its former ruler may disagree about the date when independence took place.

Country	Date of Independence	Country	Date of Independence
Antigua & Barbuda	1981	Guyana	1966
Argentina	1816	Haiti	1804
Bahamas	1973	Honduras	1838
Barbados	1966	Jamaica	1962
Belize	1981	Mexico	1821
Bolivia	1825	Nicaragua	1838
Brazil	1822	Panama	1903
Chile	1818	Paraguay	1811
Colombia	1810	Peru	1821
Costa Rica	1821	St. Kitts & Nevis	1983
Cuba	1899	St. Lucia	1979
Dominica	1967	St. Vincent & the Grenadines	1979
Dominican Republic	1844	Suriname	1975
Ecuador	1830	Trinidad and Tobago	1976
El Salvador	1821	Uruguay	1825
Grenada	1974	Venezuela	1821
Guatemala	1839		

BOLÍVAR AND SAN MARTÍN

In the early 1800s, many people in South America wanted independence from Spain. The courageous and daring Simón Bolívar (1783–1830) became the leader of Venezuela's fight for freedom in 1810. He won freedom for the northern part of the continent, including present-day Colombia, Ecuador, Panama, Peru, and Bolivia, which was named after him. José de San Martín (1778–1850) led the fight for freedom to the south. He defeated Spanish armies in Argentina, Chile, and Peru. By 1825, Spain had given up all of its South American territory.

Natural Features

Middle and South America can be divided into three smaller areas: 1) Mexico and Central America, 2) South America, and 3) the Caribbean. Mexico and Central America runs from the U.S.-Mexican border to the Panama-Colombia border—a distance of about 2,500 miles (4,025 kilometers). Although known for its spectacular coastline, this is primarily a mountainous region. There are two major ranges in Mexico, the Sierra Madre Occidental to the west and the Sierra Madre Oriental to the east. They meet as they near Central America to form the **highlands** from Guatemala to Panama. In Mexico, there is a wide central plateau. Much of Central America is an **isthmus** connecting North and South America.

The mountains continue down through South America as the Andes Mountains, which border the continent's west coast. To the east, the mountains slope down into rolling highlands that make up much of the northern portion of South America. In the central portion of the continent, near the equator, water from the surrounding mountains flows into the warm and humid Amazon basin and its millions of acres of lush rain forest. In the southern portion of South America, the mountains flatten into vast grasslands called the Pampas.

The third area, the Caribbean, stretches from the Gulf of Mexico to the Atlantic Ocean. These islands were created by volcanoes or by coral formations. They cover an area that measures more than 2,000 miles (3,220 kilometers) at its longest point.

← The Soufriere Hills volcano on Montserrat is one of the stunning natural features of the region. The ash from its eruption in 1997 covered an enormous area (see page 16).

Major bodies of water

Middle and South America form a barrier between the Atlantic Ocean and Pacific Ocean that covers more than half the distance between the North Pole and the South Pole. Until a canal system was completed through Panama in 1914, ships had to sail around the southern tip of South America to reach one ocean from the other. The Panama Canal reduced the length of such trips by up to 8,000 miles (12,875 kilometers).

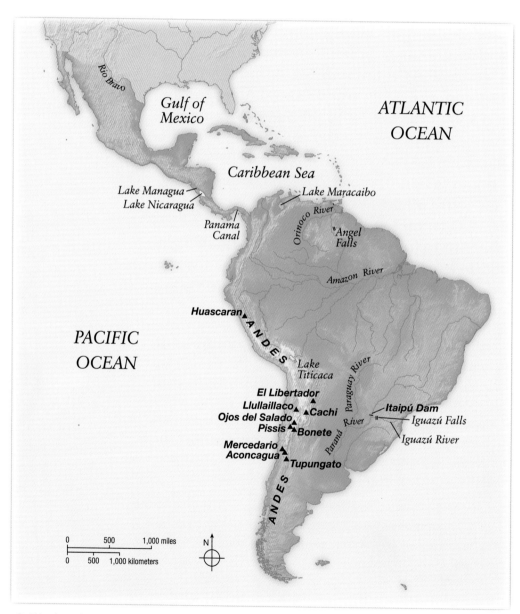

This physical map of the region shows its major rivers, lakes, and tallest mountain peaks.

The Gulf of Mexico measures about 615,000 square miles (1.6 million square kilometers). It is rich in food and natural resources, including oil and natural gas. There is evidence in the Gulf of Mexico of a major meteor impact from about 65 million years ago. Scientists believe that this impact may have triggered the events that led to the extinction of the dinosaurs.

The Caribbean Sea is located to the south of the Gulf of Mexico. It is separated from the Atlantic Ocean by the island nations that form the eastern edge of the Caribbean Plate, which is one of the region's major geological features. The Caribbean Sea covers an area of about 1 million square miles (2.6 million square kilometers). This body of water takes its name from the Carib people who once populated many of its islands.

The region's other major bodies of water include Lake Managua and Lake Nicaragua in Nicaragua, Lake Titicaca in Bolivia and Peru, and Lake Maracaibo in Venezuela. Each is important to the culture and economy of the region. The lakes provide food, transportation, and in some cases drinking water to the millions who live nearby.

At 12,500 feet (3,810 meters) above sea level, Lake Titicaca is the world's highest lake that ships can sail through. It forms part of the border between Bolivia and Peru in the Andes Mountains. There are more than three dozen islands on Lake Titicaca, some of which support large populations. The lake also has more than 40 islands that are made of floating reeds. These human-made islands are home to the Uros people, who have been living there for hundreds of years. The Uros originally created the islands to escape Peru's powerful Incan Empire.

THE PANAMA CANAL

The region's most important waterway is the Panama Canal, which enables ships to cross from the Atlantic Ocean to the Pacific Ocean without traveling around the tip of South America. This saves time, money, and lives. The Panama Canal was completed by the United States in 1914 and is 50 miles (82 kilometers) long. Starting in the 1950s, the people of Panama began demanding that their country should own and operate the canal instead of the United States. In 1977, a treaty was signed to begin this process. In 1999, Panama officially took possession of the canal. Between 35 and 50 ships pass through the Panama Canal on a typical day. A proposed plan to widen the canal would enable the largest cargo ships to pass through its locks.

Rivers

The rivers of South America are its lifelines. Hundreds of rivers snake down from the mountains into highland and lowland areas, providing power for cities, irrigation for farms, and fresh water for drinking. The Amazon River, which begins in Peru and flows through Brazil to the Atlantic Ocean, is more than 4,000 miles (6,435 kilometers) long and has more than 500 **tributaries**. During the rainy season, parts of the river are 20 miles (32 kilometers) wide. One-fifth of the total volume of fresh water entering the world's oceans comes from the Amazon. One can travel many miles into the Atlantic from the mouth of the river and still pull drinkable fresh water from the sea. The Amazon also supports an amazing ecosystem, and is one of the most important natural areas on Earth. One-tenth of the world's plants and animals live in the Amazon River basin, many of them rare. The trees in the Amazon basin convert millions of tons of carbon dioxide into oxygen each year, which is why this area has been called the Lungs of the Earth.

Among the region's other important waterways are the Orinoco River and the Paraná River. The Orinoco cuts through Venezuela from west to east. One of its tributaries leads to Angel Falls, the world's highest waterfall at 3,212 feet (979 meters) tall. The falls are named after explorer Jimmy Angel, who first brought the falls to the world's attention in the 1930s. The Paraná River flows south through Brazil, Paraguay, and Argentina, supplying power to all three countries. It is the site of the Itaipú Dam, built in the 1970s and 1980s. The Itaipú Dam is currently the largest **hydroelectric** station in the world, but new, larger ones are being built. The Paraná meets with other major rivers, including the Iguazú River and Paraguay River. Iguazú Falls, on the Brazil-Argentina border, is a series of more than 250 falls and is one of the most breathtaking sights in South America.

CITY ON A LAKE

Before the arrival of Europeans, the largest city in the New World was Tenochtitlán, where more than 200,000 Aztec people lived. Tenochtitlán was built in the center of Lake Texcoco and could only be reached by boat or across narrow paths above the water. Today, the lakebed is dry and Mexico City stands on the site of the ancient city. Earthquakes that strike Mexico City often cause massive destruction because the shaking earth can cause the dried mud to become extremely unstable.

Among the river systems in Central America and Mexico, the most important is the Rio Grande, which forms the border between Mexico and the United States. In Mexico, it is called the Rio Bravo.

The Longest Rivers in Middle and South America

River	Approximate Length in miles (kilometers)
Amazon	3,912 (6,296)
Paraná	2,795 (4,498)
Madeira	2,012 (3,238)
Purus	1,993 (3,207)
São Francisco	1,987 (3,198)
Rio Grande (Rio Bravo)	1,885 (including distance in U.S.) (3,034)
Tocantins	1,677 (2,700)
Paraguay	1,584 (2,550)
Japurá	1,500 (2,414)
Orinoco	1,281 (2,062)
Pilcomayo	1,242 (2,000)

Mountains

The Andes Mountains run the entire length of South America. At 5,500 miles (8,900 kilometers) long, it is the longest mountain chain on Earth. The tallest peak is Aconcagua in Argentina, which rises 22,834 feet (6,960 meters) above sea level. The Andes are part of a system that continues up through Central and North America, right into Alaska. In Mexico, the chain splits into the eastern and western Sierra Madres. Between them is a plateau, which is home to most of the country's people.

The mountains of Middle and South America are part of a geologically active region. In Central America, the rich soil deposited by ancient volcanoes enables millions of people to farm in the highlands. Elsewhere in the region, violent earthquakes have caused destruction by toppling buildings and triggering gigantic mud slides.

The Andes is longest mountain range in the world. Many of its most impressive peaks, including these, are in Chile.

Living on the edge

It is easy to forget that many countries in the Caribbean are actually the tops of mountains poking out of the water. The people of Montserrat, a British territory about 300 miles (480 kilometers) southeast of Puerto Rico, received a deadly reminder of this in 1995, when the Soufriere Hills volcano began spewing ash over the southern and central parts of the island. As the volcano increased in power, more and more people were affected. In 1997, the town of Plymouth, Montserrat's capital, had to be evacuated, and within a year, it was totally destroyed (see page 10). Fewer than 10,000 people remained on the island. Most of Montserrat's residents became refugees, with many moving to Antigua and others seeking new homes in Great Britain.

The Ten Tallest Peaks in Middle and South America

Mountain	Country	Height in feet (meters)
Aconcagua	Argentina	22,834 (6,960)
Ojos del Salado	Argentina	22,664 (6,908)
Bonete	Argentina	22,546 (6,872)
Tupungato	Argentina	22,310 (6,800)
Pissis	Argentina	22,241 (6,779)
Mercedario	Argentina/Chile	22,211 (6,770)
Huascaran	Peru	22,205 (6,768)
Llullaillaco	Argentina/Chile	22,057 (6,723)
El Libertador	Argentina	22,047 (6,720)
Cachi	Argentina	22,047 (6,720)

Machu Picchu

Almost 1,000 years ago, the Inca people built a vast empire that they ruled from the mountains of Peru. They built nearly 12,500 miles (20,000 kilometers) of roads and constructed aqueducts to bring water to their cities. The most famous Incan city is Machu Picchu, built high in the Andes Mountains.

Machu Picchu was a magnificent city built in the mountains of Peru by the Incas. Today, it is a top tourist attraction.

Islands

There are more island republics in the Caribbean Sea than anywhere else in the world—thirteen in all. The United States, United Kingdom, France, and the Netherlands also control island territories in the region. Most Caribbean islands are covered by tropical forests and have beautiful sandy beaches. They are popular tourist destinations and produce much of the region's sugar, coffee, and tobacco. The largest island nations are Cuba (about 11.4 million people), Dominican Republic (9.2 million), Haiti (8.3 million), Jamaica (2.8 million), and Trinidad and Tobago (1.1 million). The U.S. territory of Puerto Rico has a population of about 3.9 million.

Among the most interesting islands in Middle and South America are the Galapagos Islands and Easter Island, both located in the Pacific Ocean. The Galapagos, which belong of Ecuador, mark the place where scientist Charles Darwin first developed his theory of evolution. He noticed that birds and reptiles had developed special adaptations to the different environments of the 10 major islands. Easter Island, which belongs to Chile, is famous for the haunting Maoi statues that keep watch over its coastline.

The Galapagos marine iguana is the only sea-going lizard in the world.

BAHAMAS

ATLANTIC OCEAN

CUBA

WEST INDIES

HAITI

DOMINICAN REPUBLIC

GUADELOUPE (Fr.)

JAMAICA

Puerto Rico (U.S.)

MARTINIQUE (Fr.)

DOMINICA

Caribbean Sea

BARBADOS

ST. LUCIA

NETHERLANDS ANTILLES (Neth.)

GRENADA

TRINIDAD & TOBAGO

N

0   250 miles

0   250 kilometers

CENTRAL AMERICA

SOUTH AMERICA

This map shows the island nations located in the Caribbean Sea.

The Falkland Islands lie in the South Atlantic Ocean, off the coast of Argentina. They are a self-governing territory of the United Kingdom. However, Argentina has also claimed ownership of the Falkland Islands since the 1800s. In 1982, Argentina invaded this territory. Great Britain sent troops to liberate the islands and defeated the Argentine military. In 2007, Argentina reasserted its demand to control the Falklands.

PUERTO RICO

One of the most important centers for business, banking, and tourism in the Caribbean region is Puerto Rico, which lies 1,000 miles (1,600 kilometers) southeast of Miami, Florida. It is among the many territories in the Caribbean that are governed by other nations. Puerto Rico is a commonwealth of the United States. Its citizens enjoy most of the benefits of U.S. citizenship, including the right to travel freely within the 50 states, but they do not pay U.S. taxes. Some Puerto Ricans want their homeland to become America's 51st state so they can participate in presidential elections and be represented in the U.S. Congress. Others believe that Puerto Rico deserves to be its own independent country.

Climate

Middle and South America includes some of the wettest, driest, warmest, coldest, and windiest places on Earth. The Amazon basin receives more than 80 inches (203 centimeters) of rain each year, while the deserts of Chile and Mexico receive almost none. Every few years, a warm ocean current swirls along the western coast of South America and creates a dramatic climate change called **El Niño**. Dry regions receive heavy rainfall, while other places experience terrible droughts.

The weather in most Caribbean countries is sunny and pleasant, a big reason why people from all over the world vacation there. However, during the summer and fall, tropical storms often spin their way through the Caribbean and the Gulf of Mexico. When these storms strengthen and become hurricanes, they can devastate the region's island nations, as well as portions of Mexico, Belize, Guatemala, and Honduras.

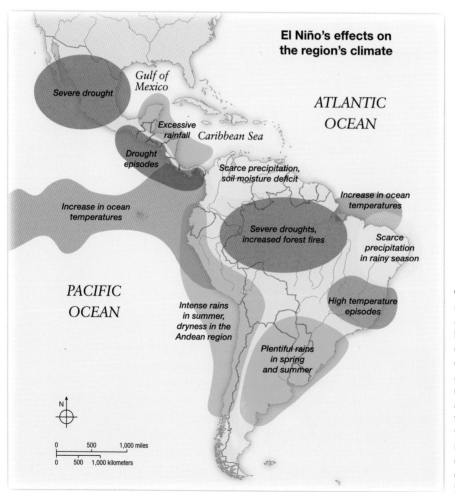

El Niño's effects on the region's climate

Gulf of Mexico

Severe drought

Excessive rainfall

Caribbean Sea

ATLANTIC OCEAN

Drought episodes

Scarce precipitation, soil moisture deficit

Increase in ocean temperatures

Increase in ocean temperatures

Severe droughts, increased forest fires

Scarce precipitation in rainy season

PACIFIC OCEAN

Intense rains in summer, dryness in the Andean region

High temperature episodes

Plentiful rains in spring and summer

N

0   500   1,000 miles
0   500   1,000 kilometers

← The warming conditions of El Niño are natural and have been happening for centuries. The opposite, cooling effect is known as La Niña. The patterns of these two trends are irregular, but they tend to run in three- to six-year cycles. This map shows the effect of El Niño on the climate of Middle and South America.

HELLO MUMMY

Although both countries border the Pacific Ocean, portions of Ecuador and Peru are among the driest places on Earth. Centuries ago, the ancient inhabitants buried their dead in underground chambers or in high caves, where their bodies were naturally dried and preserved. These mummies were bundled in beautiful textiles, with their important possessions wrapped around them. As the cities in the region grow, mummy bundles are often unearthed by builders. The race is on to stay one step ahead of the bulldozers and preserve these important artifacts.

Hurricane!

From June to November, the warm, sunny weather of the Caribbean is sometimes interrupted by violent tropical storms called hurricanes. High winds, heavy rain, and great tidal surges cause great damage and loss of life. During the worst storms, winds can reach 150 mph (241 kph) or more. Hurricanes form off the coast of Africa and move through the Caribbean in unpredictable ways. They often continue on to strike the coast of Mexico or the United States.

This tropical rainstorm is falling over the rain forest in the Guyana Highlands in Venezuela.

People

The story of Middle and South America can be told through the blending of its many cultures over the centuries. Long before Europeans arrived, mighty kingdoms rose and fell, and with each there was a sharing of art, science, and traditions among the people of different lands. After indigenous people made contact with European settlers, the mixing of cultures and sharing of customs became even more widespread.

In some cases, this had a devastating effect on indigenous populations. The people of the Caribbean were wiped out by disease and warfare brought by the Spanish. Only a small population of Carib—the people who inhabited many of the islands controlled by the Spanish—survives on the island of Dominica. In other cases, the ancient cultures were able to resist drastic change. In parts of Brazil and Mexico, and in many mountainous sections of the region, life remained largely unchanged. However, the new cultures that emerged in much of the region formed their own identities, separate from Europe and separate from the ancient ways. This new sense of identity was at the heart of the independence movements of the early 1800s, when many of today's countries broke away from their Spanish and Portuguese **colonial** rulers.

Today, the rhythm of life in most of Middle and South America is a blend of native cultures and Spanish customs. Although Spanish-speaking people are often grouped together by outsiders, dramatic differences exist between the people in each region and often within each country, too. What most have in common is a deep religious faith and a desire for a better future.

← The July 2006 elections in Mexico were hotly contested. Supporters of candidate Andrés Manuel López Obrador, like those seen here, demanded a recount after his opponent Felipe Calderón was declared the winner.

Religions

The Mayan, Incan, and Aztec civilizations had very complex religions. All were closely tied to the cycles of the sun, moon, and stars. Each religion included the practice of sacrificing animals, and sometimes humans, to their gods. The Mayans had several important gods, but their principal god was Gemma, who stood for love and passion. The main god of the Incas was Inti, the sun god. Much of the information about Incan religion was lost when Spanish missionaries burned the civilization's *khipus*, the knotted cords that were used for record-keeping. The Aztecs worshipped several gods, including Tlaloc and Huitzilopochtli. Tlaloc was the god of rain and fertility. Huitzilopochtli, who was often represented as a hummingbird, was the god of war and the god of the sun.

When the Spanish conquered the native people of South America, Central America, and Mexico, they convinced them to give up their belief systems and convert to Catholicism. In some cases, this switch was done willingly. In other cases, the people were forced to do so.

Many centuries later, Catholicism remains the major religion in the region. Most countries are 80 to 90 percent Catholic. However, some customs and symbols from the ancient cultures still play an important part in church ceremonies.

Countries in Middle and South America in which religions other than Catholicism flourish include Guyana and Suriname. Both have large populations of **Hindus** and **Muslims**. After slavery was outlawed in the 1800s, the need for agricultural workers drew many people from South Asia, where **Hinduism** and **Islam** are the two main religions. They made the long journey hoping for better wages and a chance to own land. Today, about half of Guyanans are of Indian descent. In Suriname, about half the people can claim ancestors from India, Indonesia, and China.

In the Caribbean, most of the 35 million residents are members of one of the many Christian faiths. As on the mainland, the main religious branch in each country is closely related to that of the European power that first colonized it. For example, the majority of Jamaicans describe themselves as **Protestant**. This is also true among the people of Great Britain, Jamaica's previous colonial ruler.

Because many of the Caribbean island nations are crossroads for world trade, other faiths have flourished in the region. Some people have rediscovered traditional African religions or religions that developed among African slaves and their descendants. The Caribbean is also home to many Muslims, Hindus, and Jews.

CELEBRATE!

In Middle and South America, it seems as if there is a national festival going on somewhere almost every week of the year. Most are connected to major religious holidays, but some celebrate important agricultural dates or historical occurrences. In Barbados, Crop Over is a five-week party of parades and concerts that takes place each summer. This tradition dates back to the harvest time of the sugarcane crop. In Mexico, the entire country celebrates Cinco de Mayo (Fifth of May). It marks the day in 1862 when the people of Mexico expelled the French army and affirmed their independence once and for all to the world.

For many people in Middle and South America, Carnival is a time when religion and culture come together in an explosion of color, music, and dancing. This celebration, which usually includes an elaborate parade, takes place right before Lent, a solemn period in the Catholic faith that leads up to Easter.

Children enjoy these sugar skull candies as part of the Day of the Dead festivities. Despite its name, the Day of the Dead is a joyful Mexican holiday, whose roots can be traced back to Aztec times.

Government

Most of the people in Middle and South America live under governments based on models in North America and Europe. Most vote for their leaders or have some say in who runs the government. During much of the 20th century this was not the case, however, as many countries were ruled by dictators who took power by force. As recently as the 1980s, Argentina, Bolivia, Brazil, Chile, El Salvador, Guatemala, Haiti, Honduras, Panama, Paraguay, Peru, Suriname, and Uruguay had military leaders.

For much of the 20th century, the government of the United States supported the military leaders of the region. Even those who were cruel or unfair to their people often enjoyed American aid. The United States influenced the governments of Middle and South America to protect American businesses and later to fight the threat of Communism.

Today, the region's democratic leaders face the challenges caused by soaring populations, underperforming economies, lack of education, and primitive infrastructure. Traditionally, they have depended on tourism and natural resources to keep their countries running, but often this is not enough. The low pay received by many government officials also leads to problems of corruption.

In many of the region's countries, the people have begun supporting leaders who view old allies such as the United States with suspicion and anger. During the 1900s, American businesses often meddled in political and cultural affairs with little regard for the welfare of the people. Today, political leaders such as Venezuela's Hugo Chávez believe that the United States and other world powers still view them as countries to be **exploited**. Such leaders believe that their countries would be better served by strengthening political and economic bonds within the region.

Urbanization

Although many people prefer the traditional village life, they cannot always produce enough food or make enough money to live from year to year. Beginning about 50 years ago, many country folk, or *campesinos*, started moving to the cities, where work is steadier and more opportunities can be found.

Unfortunately, almost all of the region's cities have become overcrowded and can no longer provide jobs or housing for all of their residents. While many people have found the comfortable life they sought, many more are worse off than ever. Dealing with the problems of poverty, crime, and homelessness in the cities may be the greatest challenge for the future leaders of Middle and South America.

Rio de Janeiro in Brazil is known as a luxury vacation spot, but it is also a city with many poor people. Such contrasts can make politics in the region volatile.

Agriculture

Land is the most precious resource in Middle and South America, yet not all land that could be devoted to growing food is used in a productive way. In the past, some governments in the region believed that the land would be more productive if small farms were allowed to flourish. The thinking was that farmers would work harder and produce more food if they owned the land. This was not the case. Such programs slowed the introduction of new agricultural techniques and technologies, as many traditional farmers were reluctant to accept change.

These village fishermen in Honduras are casting their nets for wild shrimp, in a lagoon shared with shrimp farmers.

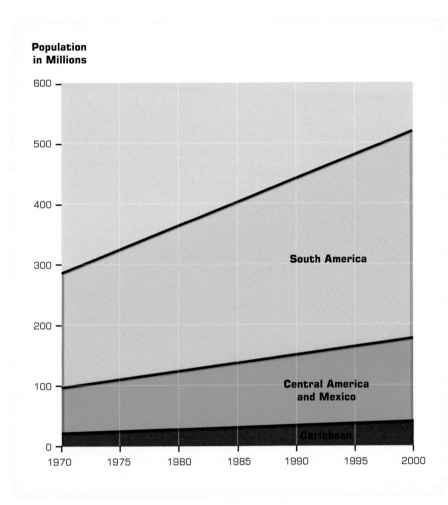

Population in Millions

600 —

500 —

400 —

300 — **South America**

200 —

100 — **Central America and Mexico**

0 — **Caribbean**

1970   1975   1980   1985   1990   1995   2000

As this graph shows, from 1970 to 2000 the population of Middle and South America grew by about 80 percent.

In some places, including the Amazon rain forest, these programs led to severe environmental damage. When farmers clear rain forest areas, the same land cannot be planted year after year without "resting." Many farmers simply moved on to the next patch of rain forest and cut it down to create a new field. Combined with the land that was cleared for cattle ranching, the amount of Amazon rain forest lost each year rose to more than 7,500 square miles (19,425 square kilometers) in the 1990s. Efforts to slow the clearing of the rain forest have met with some success, but environmental experts argue that even greater strides must be made. The Amazon rain forest helps control the amount of carbon dioxide in the atmosphere and also cools the air that flows through it—both important weapons in the fight against **global warming**.

Culture

Middle and South America is an enormous region with greatly varying geography and extremely diverse cultures. For the most part, these cultures are a mix of Native American, European, and African influences. The "ingredients" differ greatly from country to country, however, and in many cases there are stark differences between the lifestyles of people living just a few miles apart.

As technology and travel bring the people of the world closer together, the cultures of Middle and South America have begun changing very rapidly. The latest U.S. clothing and music, for example, quickly find their way into even the most remote towns through increased contact with the outside world. Of course, the outside world is also discovering the diverse flavors, sounds, and styles of these once-remote places.

Cultural pride and national identity take many forms in this vast region. For example, the people of Chile call their country the Land of Poets. Poetry is enjoyed by Chileans of all ages and from every part of society. The country's best-known poets are Pablo Neruda and Gabriela Mistral. Argentina is famous for its cultural traditions of music and dance. These forces come together in the tango, a dramatic dancing style that celebrates romance and love.

← Marketplaces in villages, such as this one in Pisac, Peru, are important for both social and economic reasons.

CHOCOLATE AND COWBOYS

Two of the earliest worldwide cultural influences to come from Middle and South America were chocolate and cowboys. Cocoa, which was used as a flavoring in Native American cooking, was unknown to most Europeans before the 1500s. Once mixed with milk and sugar, cocoa became chocolate and was a worldwide sensation. The symbol of American freedom and adventure—the cowboy—was modeled on the gauchos who tended cattle from Argentina to Mexico in the early 1800s.

Culture of Mexico and Central America

Many of the people of Mexico and Central America are descended from the native people of the region, as well as from European settlers. The official language is Spanish in every country but Belize, a former British colony. There, the official language is English. However, the farther one travels into the mountains and countryside, the more likely one is to hear traditional tongues. In Mexico's Yucatan, ancient Mayan is still spoken by most people. In tiny Guatemala, more than 20 distinct languages are still in use.

In recent years, the quality of education has become an important issue in Central America and Mexico. Although there are many fine universities, millions of people in rural areas and city slums still do not enjoy the benefits of basic schooling. This situation is slowly improving, and literacy rates are on the rise. In Costa Rica, Panama, and Mexico, the literacy rate has risen

This diver is exploring the coral reefs off Cozumel Island in Mexico.

to more than 90 percent. The Central American country that still lags behind is Guatemala, where only one in three women can read, but rates are higher for men.

The largest city in the northern part of Middle and South America is Mexico City. Because the area is prone to earthquakes, most people live and work in buildings that are only a couple of stories tall. The city has grown out instead of up, which means that people live far from their jobs. With millions of cars jamming Mexico City's narrow streets, pollution has become a major problem. To make matters worse, the city is built in a valley that traps pollution. Similar problems are plaguing other large cities in Mexico and Central America.

OCEAN VIEW

For much of the 20th century, wealthy foreigners bought Mexico's most beautiful seaside property. The government passed a law prohibiting foreign buyers, hoping that the coastline would forever belong to the Mexican people. However, foreigners still buy up much of the land through bank trusts. In this type of transaction, a Mexican bank still owns the land, but the foreign buyer is the only person allowed to use it.

↑ The Panama Canal is the world's most important shipping channel. Panama took over control of the canal from the United States in 1999. Many aspects of the canal are undergoing a modernization program.

These Puerto Ricans in New York City are celebrating the annual Puerto Rican Day Parade.

Culture of the Caribbean

The pace of life in most Caribbean countries is dictated by agriculture and tourism. The soil on the islands is quite **fertile**, and most crops can be grown all year long. Many of the world's favorite spices come from the Caribbean. The region's climate also makes it a popular destination for vacationers from North America, South America, and Europe. The cultures of the different Caribbean nations tend to differ based on two things: the European country that once controlled the island (or still does) and the origin of its people. Some came as immigrants from Europe, some from other regions of Latin America, and others as slaves from Africa. The island of Hispaniola is divided between the Dominican Republic and Haiti. Generally, the people of Haiti are dark-skinned and speak French. Dominicans are a mix of races and speak Spanish.

WORKING HARD

The most important business in the Caribbean is tourism. Foreign visitors generate tens of billions of dollars each year for the region's island nations. For many Caribbean economies, tourism accounts for more than half of their annual wealth. In order to compete in this marketplace, many governments have created educational programs for young people who hope to make a career in the tourism industry. Courses range from hotel management and accounting to engineering and the culinary arts.

Cuban leader Fidel Castro has been the leader of the Caribbean's largest nation for more than 45 years. This photo of him was taken in 1988.

Cuba

The largest country in the Caribbean is Cuba, which lies less than 100 miles (160 kilometers) south of the Florida Keys. About a quarter of the Caribbean region's population lives there. Cuba was a close ally of the United States for much of the 20th century, but most of its people did not benefit from this friendship. In 1959, Cubans revolted against the country's military leader, and the new leader, Fidel Castro, installed a Communist government. Under Communism, the government owns all the property and resources and distributes the resources to the people. Generally, people have less personal freedom under Communism than they do under **capitalism**.

Castro hoped to "export" Communism to other countries in the region. This made the United States very nervous, and the two countries became bitter enemies. The Cuban people were caught in the middle. They saw many of their basic freedoms disappear and suffered through food and energy shortages. Although the new government brought improvements in education and public welfare, this was not enough. Thousands of people risked their lives to escape the oppressive Castro government.

Culture of South America

South America is a large continent that borders two oceans and is divided by soaring mountains and thick jungles. The lands in the north, from Colombia across to French Guiana, feature cultures that blend a lot of Caribbean influences. The people of Guyana, for example, actually think of themselves more as West Indians than South Americans because much of their contact with neighbors is focused on the Caribbean, which is sometimes called the West Indies. To the west, cultural influences in countries such as Peru, Bolivia, and Ecuador are based on centuries-old traditions from the highland and mountain regions. Many towns are still very isolated. This can be seen in the style of dress and the ancient languages spoken by the people in these remote areas.

Buenos Aires, Argentina, is a bustling city where business and culture are thriving.

To the east, Brazil is a cultural region unto itself. Although most of its people speak Portuguese, there is much diversity within the population. Brazil has many blends of indigenous people, Africans, Europeans, and Asians. Deep in the Amazon rain forest, some cultures still have had little or no contact with the outside world, although there are fewer and fewer of these cultures today.

South and west of Brazil are Paraguay, Uruguay, Chile, and Argentina. They make up the "point" of South America. The major cities in this part of South America have a mix of cultures, while the outlying areas tend to be very quiet and traditional. In the countries along the Atlantic coast, one can still sense some influences of European culture. From the late 1800s to the mid-1900s, a steady stream of immigrants from Italy, Germany, and other parts of Europe arrived in this area.

Mestizos

Many people in South America are descended from mestizos. Years ago, this name was given to individuals who had both Spanish and Native American parents. Today, the term *mestizo* is used to describe all people who share a native and European heritage. In some countries, including Brazil, the term is also used to describe all people of mixed heritage. In other countries, *mestizo* is an official word that is used for census purposes. In Peru, the term simply applies to anyone who is not part of the traditional native culture. In South America, mestizos make up the majority of the population in Colombia, Ecuador, Paraguay, and Venezuela.

GOAL!

For the people of South America, national pride reaches a fever pitch during international soccer matches. Each country selects the best athletes from its professional clubs to play on a team of stars that represents the country. Everything comes to a halt when the national team is playing—especially when the opponent is another South American team.

South American countries have fielded some of the best clubs in soccer history. Brazil has won soccer's ultimate trophy, the World Cup, five times. Argentina has won the competition twice, as has Uruguay, which hosted the first World Cup in 1930. The World Cup has been held in South America four times, and plans are under way for Brazil to host the event in 2014.

In Mexico City, an artist is making a mosaic of Aztec designs on the Zocalo, the city's main square. Aztec symbolism remains an influence on many Mexican artists today.

Art and music

The art and music of Middle and South America brings together past and present. In Mexico and Central America, wonderful paintings and crafts are produced by village artisans who interpret ancient themes in modern styles. Mexico's most famous painters were Diego Rivera and Frida Kahlo, who were married to each other two separate times. Rivera was known for his dramatic murals, and Kahlo was known for her celebration of the lives of indigenous people.

The most popular traditional music in Mexico is *ranchera*, which is often performed by colorfully dressed mariachi bands. This style of music celebrates country life, love, nature, and patriotism.

SALSA

One of the most popular forms of music in the region is salsa. This spicy, energetic sound has its roots in Cuba, where African, European, and Spanish music came together in the 1930s and 1940s. During the 1960s, salsa found its way to the Cuban and Puerto Rican dance clubs of New York City. From there it spread throughout the world. By the 1990s, salsa was popular in dance clubs from Paris to Tokyo. The emergence of salsa increased the awareness and popularity of other forms of music from Middle and South America, and opened the way for today's international music stars.

In the Caribbean, the joyous sounds of calypso evolved from African and French influences and spread from the island of Trinidad throughout the region. Reggae, a newer style of music, began in Jamaica and borrowed from a combination of traditional and modern styles. Caribbean art is known for its vibrant colors, which celebrate life with great emotion and humor. A popular painting style in the region uses images inspired by traditional folk art to tell modern stories.

South American art differs by region and ranges from traditional to modern. The continent is perhaps best known for its music. The first explorers of the Amazon region were enchanted by instruments that mimicked the sounds of the jungle. In many countries, the gentle, haunting sound of flute music fills the air. Brazil's most famous artistic export is samba music, which originated in the streets of Rio de Janeiro about a century ago.

Food!

Many of the world's best-known and best-loved flavors come from Middle and South America. From chocolate to cinnamon to more than 100 types of peppers, the region boasts more ways to season meat, chicken, fish, fruits, and vegetables than any one person could taste

← In Argentina, meat is almost always on the menu. Traditional Argentine barbecue, shown above, has become very popular in the United States.

in a lifetime. Rice, corn, and beans form the foundation of the typical diet in most of the region's countries. Beyond these food staples, the only limits are a cook's creativity.

The cuisine of Mexico is perhaps the best known by the outside world. Mexican food differs by climate and geography. In the north, meat dishes are a specialty. The south is famous for its many styles of chicken and vegetables. Along the Caribbean, fish is seasoned with different spices and combined with fruits and vegetables. The intense flavors of Mexican cooking are a blend of pre-Columbian cooking—which included chilies, tropical fruits, chocolate, and vanilla—and Spanish cuisine, which included rice, pork, chicken, garlic, and onions.

Many of the basic foods enjoyed throughout the world originated in Middle and South America. About 10,000 years ago, the people of central Mexico began domesticating corn. By 3,000 years ago, the crop had spread throughout the region. The first potatoes were grown in the western part of South America, in modern-day Chile and Peru. Potatoes are still very important to South American cultures. The tomato is also believed to have come from this area. All of these foods spread to the rest of the world in the 1500s, after the first explorers brought samples back from the Americas.

Spice of life

Middle and South America is known for its many different chili peppers. Chilies are the fruit of the capsicum plant, which can grow in almost any environment. Although mammals feel a burning sensation when they consume the spicier chilies, birds do not. Birds eat the peppers, which are high in vitamin C, and then spread the seeds across wide areas. This is how so many varieties, more than 100, came to exist.

WRAP IT UP

People in every country from Mexico south to Argentina and Chile eat tortillas. Depending on where you are eating, however, the word *tortilla* can mean two very different things. In Mexico and the Central American countries, a tortilla is a flat, unleavened bread made of corn flour or wheat flour. In most of South America, a tortilla is a large omelette made of eggs, thinly sliced potatoes, chopped onions, and local spices. This type of tortilla is sliced like a pizza and eaten at room temperature.

Natural Resources and Economy

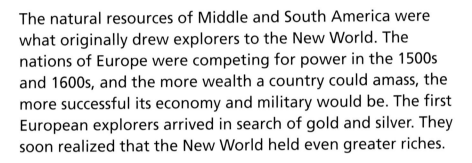

The natural resources of Middle and South America were what originally drew explorers to the New World. The nations of Europe were competing for power in the 1500s and 1600s, and the more wealth a country could amass, the more successful its economy and military would be. The first European explorers arrived in search of gold and silver. They soon realized that the New World held even greater riches.

In time, almost every European country established colonies in Middle and South America. Their goal was to exploit the region's mineral resources and to develop new sources of food and raw materials to send back to Europe. In many cases, the indigenous people were encouraged (or forced) to work in industries that made life easier for the people back in Europe, but that brought hardship and misery to their own villages.

Today, the economies of Middle and South America are diverse and sophisticated. Mexico produces many different minerals, as well as lumber, oil, and natural gas. The Central American nations and the Caribbean countries export important agricultural products, including sugar, cotton, cocoa, coffee, spices, and citrus fruits. In South America, the forests provide lumber and important medicines. Off the continent's western coast, the Pacific Ocean is teeming with fish that are caught commercially. Coffee is an important crop in Colombia and Brazil, and beef and wheat are major exports for Argentina.

← This oil tower is in Barinas, Venezuela. Oil is one of the many natural resources of Venezuela. Extracting it, however, has a harmful effect on the environment.

This sugarcane was grown in the Dominican Republic for export. It is being harvested mechanically.

Agriculture

With so much fertile land and so many mouths to feed, the countries of Middle and South America have always made agriculture a top priority. Because the climates vary greatly in this part of the world, crops that flourish in one country may be difficult to grow in another. In order to make the widest variety of foods available to the people, nations in the region must actively trade with their neighbors and with the rest of the world, too.

The choice of what to grow is not always an easy one. If the climate and geography make a crop such as coffee easy to raise, then farmers naturally want to raise coffee. If coffee prices are high, the nation benefits because the crop brings in money to buy the foods the nation cannot grow itself. If coffee prices drop, the country may not have enough money to buy the foods it needs. That is why governments in this region try to achieve agricultural balance.

GOING GLOBAL

With a warm climate and an almost limitless amount of land, Brazil has set its sights on becoming a world agricultural power. Already the world's top producer of sugar, Brazil hopes to be number one in coffee, juice oranges, beef, and soybeans, too. For this to happen, Brazil will need to improve its roads, railroads, and ports. It takes three times longer to ship products out of Brazil than out of many competing agricultural countries.

Among the best-known agricultural products in the region are bananas. Bananas originated in Southeast Asia and were brought to the region by Portuguese traders. Today, they are grown on enormous plantations and are one of the region's most important export crops. Ecuador, Colombia, and Costa Rica each ship more than a million tons of bananas around the world each year. An increasingly important crop in the region is soybeans. They too originated in Asia but were not planted widely in South America until the 1900s. Today, Brazil, Paraguay, Bolivia, and Argentina are among the top soybean producers in the world.

The choice of where to grow can also be a difficult one. In Brazil, thousands of square miles of rain forest are being destroyed each year to make room for more soybean farms. The cattle industry, which used to be restricted to the grassy Pampas, has expanded north, deep into Brazil, where even more rain forest is being cleared.

This boy is adding organic compost to cabbage plants in Nicaragua. The country is seeking to develop new crops other than coffee. Organic farming is becoming an important agricultural issue throughout the world.

Natural resources

After winning their independence, the countries of Middle and South America typically concentrated on establishing themselves in the world economy by exporting their most abundant resources. In Venezuela, where oil is plentiful, this strategy worked well. In Bolivia, where tin was a major export, it did not. In the years between World War I and World War II, demand for tin plummeted, and Bolivia's economy was nearly destroyed. In Chile, which depended greatly on its copper industry, falling prices during the 1980s created great economic hardship for the people.

The most successful countries have been the ones that use their mineral wealth to develop other industries. For example, Jamaica has a tremendous amount of bauxite, which is used to make aluminum. The country also produces sugar, bananas, and coffee and has a busy tourism industry. These industries produce enough wealth for the country to offer jobs, social services, and an education to almost every citizen.

In Central and South America, water is a valuable industrial resource. The rivers that cascade from the region's mountains power numerous hydroelectric plants, which in turn provide energy for homes and businesses. Without this resource, it would be difficult for their economies to grow. Running the region's most impressive hydroelectric project, the Itaipú Dam, requires the cooperation of three countries— Brazil, Paraguay, and Argentina. It would take more than 400,000 barrels

BIG CATCH

The Pacific Ocean is a rich resource for the fishing fleets of Middle and South America. Many species of edible fish are caught and shipped to the United States, and others are used for food and fertilizer by the people of the region. In parts of Peru and Chile, where the climate is too dry for farming, many people make their living in the fishing industry.

With demand for fish at an all-time high, there is a danger that some species will be **overfished**, upsetting the natural balance of the Pacific. For example, many restaurant chefs consider the Chilean sea bass to be the "perfect" fish. It tastes good, keeps a long time, and is easy to cook. Its popularity in the 1980s and 1990s led to overfishing, and now the species is in decline. The sea bass, which is caught in the frigid southern waters off Chile, takes a long time to reproduce. If catches are not limited, marine scientists believe the population will soon die out.

of oil to generate the amount of energy the dam generates each day. Beneath the earth in Mexico are some of the world's richest deposits of silver, gold, copper, and iron ore. The country also has an enormous amount of natural gas, oil, and coal.

The Itaipú Dam is the world's largest hydroelectric plant. It is run as a partnership between Brazil, Paraguay, and Argentina.

Tourism

One of the most important industries in Middle and South America is tourism. Each country does its best to convince vacationers from North America, Australia, Asia, and Europe that it is a unique, exciting, and exotic destination. The most successful countries are the island nations of the Caribbean, which offer warm weather and white-sand beaches. Some have been catering to tourists for a century or more.

The Caribbean is also a very popular destination for cruise ships. They "hop" from port to port, which enables their passengers to experience many different island cultures in just a few days. Puerto Rico has become one of the world's busiest harbors for cruise ships.

Many tourists prefer the excitement, culture, and nightlife of the region's cities, including Caracas, Rio de Janeiro, Santo Domingo, and Buenos Aires. This has made many of the urban areas of Middle and South America popular destinations, too.

The islands of the Caribbean are popular stops for tourists aboard cruise ships.

← This deep-sea fishing boat is trawling for shrimp in the Gulf of Mexico.

Two new types of tourism are beginning to flourish in the region. Ecotourism, in which visitors live in harmony with the natural environment and explore their surroundings, has become extremely popular in Central American countries such as Costa Rica. One of the most popular ecotourism destinations is the Galapagos Islands, off the coast of Ecuador. Also, in South America, tourists can now join archaeological expeditions and search for clues to the region's past— from 1,000-year-old civilizations to newly discovered species of dinosaurs. The dollars they spend on these trips help preserve cultural heritage and fund scientific expeditions that benefit people all over the world.

Top 10 Tourism Destinations in Middle and South America

Destination	Approximate Number of Visitors Per Year	Expenditure by Tourists
Mexico	21.9 million	$11.8 billion
Brazil	5.4 million	$3.9 billion
Argentina	3.9 million	$2.8 billion
Dominican Republic	3.7 million	$3.5 billion
Puerto Rico	3.7 million	$3.2 billion
Cuba	2.2 million	$1.9 billion
Chile	2.0 million	$1.3 billion
Uruguay	1.8 million	$600 million
Costa Rica	1.7 million	$1.6 billion
Bahamas	1.6 million	$2.1 billion

Working life

The standard of living in Middle and South America has risen steadily during the last 25 years, and people have enjoyed more freedoms than in the past. These include more access to education and employment. Many people whose families had engaged in traditional work for generations are now working in industries that are vital for continued economic growth, such as finance, communications, and energy. Because the economies in this region are closely linked, every worker—from engineers to fishermen to farmers—is part of a much bigger picture.

The gap between rich and poor is not hard to see in most of the region's major cities. This shanty town is in São Paolo, Brazil. The prosperous city center rises in the distance.

For most people in Middle and South America, life will continue to be a daily "balancing act" between tradition and progress. Cultural beliefs and customs are very important throughout the region and ties to the past are not easily broken. At the same time, people yearn for a better life and want more opportunities. They seek the advantages that modern technology has given others in the world. In the end, each country must decide on the best plan for its people, and each person must decide how he or she will contribute to that plan. Not everyone can engage in farming or other traditional jobs, and not everyone can work in a factory or an office. For Middle and South America to achieve its political and economic goals, each country must find its own balance between the past and the future.

The income gap

Closing the wide gap between the rich and poor in Middle and South America is seen as one of the paths to economic success. One way this wealth gap is measured is by comparing the percentage of a country's income earned by the richest 20 percent of the people with the percentage of that country's income earned by the poorest 20 percent. The farther apart the numbers, the wider the gap between rich and poor. Nine countries in the region, seen in the table below, rank among the 20 worst in the world.

Income Gap Between the Rich and Poor in Middle and South America

Country	Percentage of Income Earned by the Richest 20%	Percentage of Income Earned by the Poorest 20%
Brazil	64.1	2.2
Nicaragua	63.6	2.3
Paraguay	60.7	1.9
Colombia	60.9	3.0
Chile	61.0	3.3
Honduras	59.4	2.2
Guatemala	60.6	3.8
Mexico	57.4	3.5
El Salvador	56.4	3.3

Figures are from 2002.

Transportation and communications

The most important development in Middle and South America is the communications "revolution." Until very recently, millions of people were isolated from ideas and opportunities because wires could not reach them in remote or rugged areas. That began to change in the 1990s, when satellite dishes and cellular phones diminished the obstacles that geography had long imposed. In recent years, the Internet has also reached many remote communities and helped people in these areas understand that what they do and what they think truly matter to the outside world.

⬆ Satellite dishes and cell phones have increased access to other areas in the world. They have also changed the look of countries such as Venezuela. Satellite dishes cover the roofs of apartment blocks in Caracas, the capital city.

THE BEAUTY OF BRASÍLIA

One of the greatest achievements in this region is the city of Brasília, the capital of Brazil and home to more than two million people. Unlike other major cities in the region, Brasília was never a traditional population center. Until the city was founded in 1960, the land it occupies today was undeveloped. The city was designed by an urban planner named Lucio Costa. When seen from the air, Brasília looks like a butterfly.

Brasília has many wondrous architectural features, including the National Congress building and the Juscelino Kubitschek Bridge. However, Brasilia's greatest achievement is the way it connects the many sections of such a vast country. Brazil's capital is an example of how roads, rails, and telecommunications must work together in a modern infrastructure.

For the larger nations of Middle and South America, the communications revolution also includes improving the physical links between towns and cities. That means building better roads and rail lines, so that people and goods can travel quickly and safely. Mountains, jungles, and deserts make this job very difficult and expensive. However, for a country to achieve its economic potential, it is a job that must be done.

Cell Phone and Internet Use in Middle and South America

Country	Cell Phones in Use	Internet Users
Brazil	86.2 million	25.9 million
Mexico	47.5 million	18.6 million
Argentina	22.1 million	10 million
Colombia	21.9 million	4.7 million
Venezuela	12.5 million	3 million
Chile	10.6 million	6.7 million
Peru	5.6 million	4.6 million
Ecuador	6.2 million	616,000
Dominican Republic	3.6 million	938,300
Guatemala	3.3 million*	756,000
Puerto Rico	2.7 million*	1 million

* 2004 figures; all other figures are from 2005. Source: CIA World Factbook 2007

THE DARIEN GAP

To drive from northern Mexico to southern Argentina, one must take the Pan-American Highway. This network of roads was created to unite the entire region, but a 62-mile (100-kilometer) section in Panama and Colombia was never completed. This section is called the Darien Gap. The Panama side consists of fragile **wetlands**, and the Colombian side has steep mountains.

The **biodiversity** of this area is among the richest in the world. The Panamanian government does not want a road built through this area for fear that it will attract settlers who will destroy the environment. Colombia does not wish to build through its portion either. The mountainous terrain on its side of the border would present many expensive engineering challenges.

The future

When the world looks at Middle and South America, it sees a very different region than it did a century ago. Back then, Americans and Europeans viewed the area as a source of raw materials, energy, and food. Little or no thought was given to the rights or well-being of its people, who were often treated cruelly and exploited economically.

Today, the leaders of the region hope that their nations' vast resources can be developed for the benefit of the outside world, as well as for their own people. This development would bring dramatic changes to many cultures and traditions. Each country must find its own way to prosperity, and that path may not always be clear or easy to follow.

Majour Countries Receiving Foreign Investment

Country	Foreign Direct Investment (billion U.S.$)
Argentina	4.8
Brazil	18.8
Chile	8.1
Colombia	6.3
Costa Rica	1.4
Dominican Republic	1.2
Ecuador	2.1
Jamaica	0.6
Mexico	18.9
Panama	2.6
Peru	3.5
Trinidad and Tobago	0.9
Uruguay	1.4
Venezuela	-0.5

Figures are for 2006 and include some estimates. The figures exclude main financial centres such as the Cayman Islands.

MONEY FROM THE UNITED STATES

One of the most important sources of income for the economy of Mexico—and several countries in Central America and the Caribbean—is money sent home by relatives working in the United States. Their jobs are often hard, but they pay many times more than the same work in their home countries. Although many of these workers are living in the United States without permission, they fill an important role in two economies. Many people believe that new laws need to be passed to protect the rights of U.S. citizens, as well as the rights of illegal workers.

With the increased power of the region comes greater responsibility. The leaders of Middle and South America must feed, educate, and protect their people. They must also develop new economic opportunities and invest in the infrastructure of their societies. At the same time, they must protect their fragile environments and learn from the mistakes that other countries have made.

PROTECTING THE PAST

The struggle for survival in many parts of Middle and South America has led people to loot important archaeological sites and sell the artifacts to collectors. Scientists and educators in these areas have begun to work with the people to stop this practice. They try to explain that, in many cases, looters are stealing from their own ancestors. They are also teaching people how to create traditional arts and crafts that can be sold to collectors and can help promote tourism to these areas.

What does the future hold for the children of Central and South America? These Cuban children will find out soon.

Fact File

Caribbean

Country/Territory	Capital	Population	Area in square miles (sq km)
Anguilla	The Valley	13,477	37 (96)
Antigua & Barbuda	St. John's	69,108	171 (442)
Aruba	Oranjestad	71,891	75 (193)
Bahamas	Nassau	303,770	5,358 (13,878)
Barbados	Bridgetown	279,912	166 (430)
British Virgin Islands	Road Town	23,098	59 (153)
Cayman Islands	George Town	45,436	101 (262)
Cuba	Havana	11,382,820	42,804 (110,861)
Dominica	Roseau	68,910	290 (751)
Dominican Republic	Santo Domingo	9,183,984	18,730 (48,511)
Grenada	St. George's	89,703	133 (344)
Guadeloupe	Basse-Terre	452,776	658 (1,705)
Haiti	Port-au-Prince	8,308,504	10,714 (27,750)
Jamaica	Kingston	2,758,124	4,244 (10,991)
Martinique	Fort de France	436,131	425 (1,100)
Montserrat	Plymouth	9,439	39 (102)
Netherland Antilles	Willemstad	221,736	309 (800)
Puerto Rico	San Juan	3,927,188	3,427 (8,875)
St. Kitts & Nevis	Basseterre	39,129	101 (261)
St. Lucia	Castries	168,458	238 (616)
St. Vincent & the Grenadines	Kingstown	117,848	150 (388)
Trinidad and Tobago	Port-of-Spain	1,065,842	1,981 (5,130)
Turks and Caicos Islands	Grand Turk	21,152	166 (430)
U.S. Virgin Islands	Charlotte Amalie	108,605	134 (347)

Central America

Country	Capital	Population	Area in square miles (sq km)
Belize	Belmopan	287,730	8,867 (22,966)
Costa Rica	San José	4,075,261	19,730 (51,100)
El Salvador	San Salvador	6,822,378	8,124 (21,041)
Guatemala	Guatemala City	12,293,545	42,042 (108,889)
Honduras	Tegucigalpa	7,326,496	43,277 (112,088)
Nicaragua	Managua	5,570,129	50,193 (130,000)
Panama	Panama City	3,191,319	29,157 (75,517)

North America

Country	Capital	Population	Area in square miles (sq km)
Mexico	Mexico City	107,449,525	756,066 (1,958,201)

South America

Country/Territory	Capital	Population	Area in square miles (sq km)
Argentina	Buenos Aires	39,921,833	1,073,519 (2,780,400)
Bolivia	La Paz	8,989,046	424,165 (1,098,581)
Brazil	Brasília	188,078,227	3,287,613 (8,514,877)
Chile	Santiago	16,134,219	291,930 (756,096)
Colombia	Bogotá	43,593,035	439,737 (1,138,914)
Ecuador	Quito	13,547,510	109,484 (283,561)
Falkland Islands	Stanley	2,967	4,698 (12,170)
French Guiana	Cayenne	199,509	35,135 (91,000)
Guyana	Georgetown	767,245	83,000 (214,969)
Paraguay	Asunción	6,506,464	157,048 (406,752)
Peru	Lima	28,302,603	496,225 (1,285,216)
Suriname	Paramaribo	439,117	63,251 (163,820)
Uruguay	Montevideo	3,431,932	68,037 (176,215)
Venezuela	Caracas	25,730,435	352,145 (912,050)

Timeline

c.1200–400 BCE	The rise of the Olmec civilization in modern-day central Mexico.
900 CE	The rise of the Toltec civilization in modern-day Mexico.
1000	The rise of the Mayan civilization in modern-day Mexico and Central America.
1200	The rise of the Inca Empire in western South America.
1300	The rise of the Aztec Empire in modern-day south-central Mexico.
1492	Christopher Columbus lands on the island of San Salvador in the Bahamas.
1500	Pedro Álvares Cabral claims Brazil for Portugal.
1510	The Spanish establish Darien in Colombia—the first permanent European settlement on the American mainland.
1521	Hernán Cortés conquers Mexico's Aztec Empire.
1523	Pedro de Alvarado conquers Guatemala.
1532	Spanish conquistador Francisco Pizarro wins control of Inca lands in Peru.
1602	Dutch settlers land in Suriname.
1655	Great Britain seizes control of Jamaica from Spain.
1783	Simón Bolívar is born in Caracas, Venezuela, on July 24.
1680	The Portuguese begin settling Uruguay.
1804	After a slave uprising against the French, Haiti becomes the world's first black republic.
1810	Colombia declares its independence.
1816	Argentina declares its independence from Spain.
1818	Chile declares its independence from Spain.
1821	Mexico declares its independence from Spain.
1822	Brazil declares its independence.
1834	The British Empire abolishes slavery in the Caribbean.
1836	Mexico loses its northern Tejas (Texas) territory to American colonists.
1838	Costa Rica becomes a republic, starting a long tradition of democracy. It had become independent from Spain in 1821.

1845	England begins importing indentured workers from India to Trinidad and Tobago.
1879	Peru, Chile, and Bolivia start fighting the four-year War of the Pacific.
1903	Panama becomes a republic and gives the United States control over the Panama Canal.
1917	The United States purchases the Virgin Islands from Denmark.
1930	Uruguay hosts the first World Cup of soccer.
1950	Puerto Rican nationalists attempt to assassinate U.S. President Harry Truman.
1958	Jamaica leads the newly formed West Indies Federation.
1959	Fidel Castro seizes control of Cuba.
1962	Jamaica declares its independence.
1965	Cuban revolutionary Che Guevara attempts to start a civil war in Bolivia.
1966	Guyana declares its independence.
1968	The Summer Olympic Games are held in Mexico.
1969	A controversial soccer game leads to a four-day war between El Salvador and Honduras.
1973	The Bahamas declares its independence.
1979	St. Lucia declares its independence.
1981	Belize its declares independence.
1982	Argentina and Great Britain go to war over control of the Falkland Islands. After less than two months of fighting, Britain wins.
1983	U.S. forces invade Grenada to restore order after a military coup.
1988	Hurricane Gilbert, with record winds of 180 mph (290 kph), tears through the Caribbean.
1994	Mexico joins the United States and Canada in the North American Free Trade Agreement (NAFTA) and becomes a founding member of the World Trade Organization (WTO).
1997	An eruption of the Soufriere Hills volcano on Montserrat destroys the island's capital, Plymouth. Most of the island's population become refugees.
1998	Hurricane Mitch leaves 2,000 dead and many more homeless in Nicaragua.
1999	Peru and Ecuador sign a treaty that ends a 60-year border dispute. The United States hands over full control of the Panama Canal to Panama.
2000	Colombia announces a joint effort with the United States to fight the drug trade.
2006	Michelle Bachelet becomes the first female president of Chile.
2007	Venezuelan President Hugo Chávez takes control of the country's last privately run oil fields.

Glossary

biodiversity	variety of plant and animal species in an environment
capitalism	economic system based on private ownership of goods and limited government involvement
colonial	from the era when European powers controlled countries in other parts of the world
desert	very dry region with less than 1 inch (25 millimeters) of rainfall per year
El Niño	warm ocean current off the coast of Peru and Ecuador that can cause dramatic weather changes
exploited	used unfairly or selfishly
global warming	increase in the average temperature of Earth's atmosphere, caused in part by burning fossil fuels and deforestation
highlands	mountainous or elevated portion of a country
Hinduism	religion of Hindus. Hinduism involves a social system and the belief in a divine intelligence called Brahman.
hydroelectric	describes energy generated by flowing water
indigenous	native; having always been in a place
infrastructure	the basic services and systems, such as transportation, water, and schools, that enable a society to function
Islam	the religion of Muslims, based on the teachings of Muhammad and the Muslim holy book, the Koran.
isthmus	narrow strip of land connecting two larger bodies of land
metropolitan area	city and its surrounding communities
migration area	movement of a group of people or animals from one area to another
overfished	caught fish faster than they could reproduce and replenish themselves, depleting their supply
Protestant	describes Christian religions that separated from the Roman Catholic Church in the 1500s. Baptist, Presbyterian, and Lutheran are examples of Protestant religions.
treaty	agreement between two powers to end a conflict
tributary	river or stream that flows into a larger river
Tropic of Cancer	imaginary line that marks the northern edge of the tropics
Tropic of Capricorn	imaginary line that marks the southern edge of the tropics
wetlands	marshy or swampy areas

Find Out More

Further Reading

Blue, Rose and Corrine J. Naden. *Exploring Central America, Mexico, and the Caribbean.* Chicago: Raintree, 2003.

Klobuchar, Lisa. *The History and Activities of the Aztecs.* Chicago: Heinemann, 2007.

Schaffer, David. *Discovering South America's Land, People, and Wildlife.* New Jersey: Myreportlinks.com, 2004.

Organizations and Websites

www.indians.org/welker/aztec.htm
The American Indian Heritage Foundation offers information on Aztecs and Mexicas, the indigenous people of Mexico.

www.conservation.org/xp/CIWEB/regions/neotropics/
Conservation International gives information on conservation issues affecting South America.

memory.loc.gov/frd/cs/
The Library of Congress Country Studies website has profiles of more than 100 countries and regions. You can look up individual countries or browse by continent.

www.pancanal.com
The Panama Canal website offers information in both Spanish and English.

Activities

Here are some topics to research if you want to find out more about Middle and South America:

Protecting the environment

How should Brazilian farmers balance the cost of new farm equipment and technology with the environmental cost of their current methods?

Relations with other countries

Should the countries of Middle and South America concentrate more on relationships with each other or with countries such as the U.S.?

Communications technology

In what ways will cellphones, the Internet, and satellite dishes change Middle and South America?

Index

Aconcagua, Mount **15, 16**
agriculture **28–29, 34, 41, 43, 44-45**
Amazon Basin **11, 14, 20, 29, 37**
Amazon River **14, 15**
Andes Mountains **13, 15, 16, 17**
Angel Falls **14**
Anguilla **6, 8, 56**
  population **56**
Antigua & Barbuda **9, 56**
  population **56**
archaeological sites **17**
Argentina **6, 8, 9, 19, 26, 57**
  culture **31, 37**
  economy and natural resources **43, 45, 46, 49, 53, 54**
  foreign inward investment **54**
  population **57**
  tourism **49**
art **38, 39–40**
Aruba **8, 56**
  population **56**
Atlantic Ocean **12**
Aztec people **8, 14, 24, 25, 38**

Bahamas **9, 56**
  population **56**
  tourism **49**
bananas **45, 46**
Barbados **9, 25, 56**
  population **56**
bauxite **46**
Belize **9, 20, 32, 57**
  population **57**
biodiversity **53**
Bolívar, Simón **9**
Bolivia **9, 13, 26, 57**
  agriculture **45**
  culture **36**
  economy and natural resources **45, 46**
  population **57**
Brasilia **52**
Brazil **6, 9, 23, 26, 52, 57**

agriculture **45**
culture **23, 37, 40**
economy and natural resources **43, 44, 45, 46, 49, 51, 53, 54**
foreign inward investment **54**
population **57**
tourism **49**
British Virgin Islands **8, 56**
  population **56**
Buenos Aires **6, 36, 48**

calypso **39**
capitalism **35**
Caracas **48, 52**
Carib people **13, 23**
Caribbean **11, 24, 56**
culture **34–35, 39**
  islands **18–19**
  tourism **48**
Caribbean Plate **13**
Caribbean Sea **13, 18**
Carnival **25**
Castro, Fidel **35**
Catholicism **24, 25**
cattle industry **29, 32, 45**
Cayman Islands **8, 56**
  population **56**
cell phone use **52, 53**
Chávez, Hugo **26**
Chile **9, 18, 20, 26, 57**
  culture **31, 37**
  economy and natural resources **46, 49, 51, 53, 54**
  foreign inward investment **54**
  population **57**
  tourism **49**
chili peppers **41**
Christianity **24**
cities **6, 33, 48, 52**
climate **20–21, 34, 44**
coal mining **47**
cocoa and chocolate **32, 43**
coffee industry **18, 43, 44, 46**
Colombia **6, 9, 37, 53, 57**
  economy and natural

resources **43, 45, 51, 53, 54**
  foreign inward investment **54**
  population **37, 57**
colonialism **8, 43**
Communism **26, 35**
copper industry **46, 47**
coral reefs **32**
Costa Rica **9, 57**
  economy and natural resources **45, 49, 54**
  literacy **32–33**
  population **57**
  tourism **49**
cotton industry **43**
cruise ships **48**
Cuba **9, 18, 55, 56**
  culture **35, 38**
  population **56**
  tourism **49**
culture **30–41**

Darien Gap **53**
Darwin, Charles **18**
Day of the Dead **25**
deserts **20**
Dominica **9, 23, 56**
  population **56**
Dominican Republic **9, 18, 34, 56**
  economy and natural resources **44, 49, 53, 54**
  population **56**
  tourism **49**

earthquakes **14, 15, 33**
Easter Island **18**
eco-tourism **49**
economy and natural resources **26, 34, 42–55**
Ecuador **9, 18, 21, 57**
  culture **36, 37**
  economy **45, 53, 54**
  foreign inward investment **54**
  population **37, 57**
education **32–33, 34, 46**
El Niño **20**

El Salvador **9, 26, 57**
  economy **51**
  population **57**
equator **5**

Falkland Islands **8, 19, 57**
  population **57**
favelas **5**
festivals **25, 34**
fishing **28, 43, 46, 49**
food **40–41**
French Guiana **8, 57**
  population **57**

Galapagos Islands **18, 49**
gauchos **32**
gold deposits **8, 47**
governments **26**
grasslands **11**
Grenada **9, 56**
  population **56**
Guadeloupe **8, 56**
  population **56**
Guatemala **9, 20, 26, 57**
  culture **32, 33**
  economy **51, 53**
  literacy **33**
  population **57**
Gulf of Mexico **13**
Guyana **9, 24, 36, 57**
  population **57**
  religions **24**
Guyana Highlands **21**

Haiti **9, 18, 26, 34, 56**
  population **56**
Hinduism **24**
Hispaniola **34**
history of Middle and South America **8–9, 58–59**
Honduras **9, 20, 26, 28, 57**
  economy **51**
  population **57**
hurricanes **20, 21**
hydroelectricity **14, 46–47**

iguanas **18**
Iguazú Falls **14**
Iguazú River **14**

Inca people **24**
independence
    movements **8, 9, 19,
    23, 25**
industries *see* economy
    and natural resources
    infrastructure,
    underdeveloped **6, 26**
Internet **52, 53**
iron ore **47**
Islam **24**
islands **11, 18–19**
isthmus **11**
Itaipú Dam **14, 46–47**

Jamaica **9, 18, 24, 39, 56**
  agriculture **46**
  economy and natural
    resources **46, 54**
  population **56**
Japurá River **15**
Jews **24**

Kahlo, Frida **38, 39**

La Niña **20**
Lake Managua **13**
Lake Maracaibo **13**
Lake Nicaragua **13**
Lake Texcoco **14**
Lake Titicaca **13**
land ownership **28, 33**
languages **5, 32, 34, 36,
    37**
Lima **6**
literacy **33**
literature **31**
lumber trade **43**

Machu Picchu **17**
Madeira River **15**
mariachi bands **38**
markets **31**
Martinique **8, 56**
  population **56**
Maya people **24**
meat trade **40, 43**
mestizos **37**
Mexico **6, 8, 9, 11, 20,
    23, 57**
  culture **23, 32–33, 38, 41**
  economy and natural
    resources **43, 47, 49,
    51, 53, 54**
  festivals **25**
  foreign inward
    investment **54**
  literacy **32–33**

population **57**
  tourism **49**
Mexico and Central
    America region **11**
  culture **32–33, 38**
Mexico City **6, 14, 33**
military governments **26**
Mistral, Gabriela **31**
Montserrat **8, 11, 16, 56**
  population **56**
mountains **11, 15, 16, 53**
mummification **21**
music and dance **31,
    38–39, 40**

natural gas **13, 43, 47**
Neruda, Pablo **31**
Netherland Antilles **8, 56**
  population **56**
Nicaragua **9, 13, 57**
  economy **45, 50**
  population **57**

oil industry **13, 43, 46, 47**
organic farming **45**
Orinoco River **14, 15**
over-fishing **46**

Pacific Ocean **12, 18, 46**
Pampas **11, 45**
Pan-American Highway
    53
Panama **9, 26, 32, 53, 57**
  literacy **32–33**
  population **57**
Panama Canal **12, 13, 33**
Paraguay **9, 26, 57**
  agriculture **45**
  economy and natural
    resources **45, 46, 51**
  population **37, 57**
Paraguay River **14, 15**
Paraná River **14, 15**
Peru **6, 8, 9, 13, 21, 26,
    31, 57**
  culture **36, 37**
  economy and natural
    resources **46, 53, 54**
  foreign inward
    investment **54**
  population **57**
physical geography
    10–21
Pilcomayo River **15**
plants and animals **14, 18**
pollution **6, 33**
populations **6, 22–29,
    56, 57**

population growth **29**
poverty **6, 26, 27, 51**
Puerto Rico **8, 18, 19, 56**
  economy **53**
  population **56**
  tourism **48, 49**
Purus River **15**

rain forest **11, 14**
  destruction **29, 45**
rainfall **20**
ranchera **38**
reggae **39**
religions **24**
Rio Grande (Rio Bravo)
    15
Rio de Janeiro **5, 27, 48**
Rivera, Diego **38**
rivers **14–15**
road networks **53**

St. Kitts and Nevis **9,
    56**
  population **56**
St. Lucia **9, 56**
  population **56**
St. Vincent & the
    Grenadines **9, 56**
  population **56**
salsa **38**
samba **40**
San Martín, José de **9**
Santo Domingo **48**
Sáo Francisco River **15**
Sáo Paolo **6, 50**
satellite technology **52**
Sierra Madre Occidental
    11, 15
Sierra Madre Oriental
    11, 15
silver deposits **8, 47**
slavery **24, 34**
slum housing **5, 6, 50**
soccer **37**
South America **11, 57**
  culture **36–37**
soybeans **44, 45**
spices **34, 41, 43**
standards of living **50**
sugar industry **18, 25, 43,
    44, 46**
Suriname **9, 24, 26, 57**
  population **57**
  religions **24**

tango **31**
Tenochtitlán **14**
tin mining **46**

tobacco **18**
Tocantins River **15**
tortillas **41**
tourism **18, 19, 26, 34, 46,
    48–49**
transportation and
    communications
    52–53
Trinidad and Tobago **9,
    18, 39, 56**
  population **56**
Tropic of Cancer **5**
Tropic of Capricorn **5**
Turks and Caicos **8, 56**
  population **56**

United States **8, 13, 19,
    26, 31, 35, 54**
urbanization **26**
Uros people **13**
Uruguay **9, 26, 57**
  culture **37**
  population **57**
  tourism **49**
U.S. Virgin Islands **8, 56**
  population **56**

Venezuela **6, 8, 9, 13, 21,
    26, 57**
  economy and natural
    resources **43, 46, 53, 54**
  foreign inward
    investment **54**
  population **37, 57**
volcanoes **11, 15, 16**

water resources **46**
wealth gap **50, 51**
wetlands **53**
wilderness areas **7**